John of the Cross

Seasons of Prayer

IAIN MATTHEW OCD

First published 2014
Reprinted 2014

TERESIAN PRESS
Carmelite Priory
Boars Hill
Oxford OX1 5HB
priory@carmelite.org.uk

ISBN 978-0-947916-14-5

A catalogue record for this book is available
from the British Library.

Cover image © LilKar/Shutterstock.com

Cover design by Joshua Horgan, Oxford

Typeset and printed by Joshua Horgan, Oxford

For Mrs Sandra Pooley,
with gratitude for her tireless dedication
to the Carmelite Book Service

Foreword

The author, Fr Iain Matthew, OCD, needs no introduction to those who long for a deeper understanding of the teaching of St John of the Cross. He is the author of the highly acclaimed *The Impact of God: Soundings from St John of the Cross*, already translated into several languages. The current book, *John of the Cross: Seasons of Prayer*, collects in a single volume articles previously published in *Mount Carmel: A Review of the Spiritual Life*. Teresian Press is now publishing them again, in response to popular demand, making them available to an even wider readership.[1]

Thomas Merton once said: 'There is no member of the Church who does not owe something to Carmel.' Or, indeed, we could well add, to the Carmelite saints. But possibly to none more so than to the commanding figure of John of the Cross whose teaching on prayer is the subject of this book. We may even expand and qualify Merton's words, to say that there is almost certainly no competent spiritual writer today who does not look to John for light and guidance as the final word on the more sensitive and delicate regions of the human spirit in search of God.

This is not solely because he is a Doctor of the Church and so has a message approved officially for all times and all peoples. It is because he speaks from the depths of his personal experience of God, supported by a prayerful reading of the Scriptures and a deep knowledge of the human heart. His writings remain a perennial spring which continues to slake the deepest thirst of the human spirit for an authentic relationship with God in prayer.

In the pages of this book, we listen to John's voice speaking to us, encouraging us, enlightening us and drawing us ever more deeply into the mystery of Christian prayer. In a clear, limpid and engaging style, Iain Matthew explores four essential aspects of John's teaching. He begins by showing us that prayer is relationship, the presence of one person to the other – and that being with God, the Beloved, in prayer is a real possibility. This is the important message brought to us in the opening chapter. The author then goes on to explain, in the following one, how John invites us to enter the 'desert' of our needs as a place of prayer, to stay there, to take these needs before the Lord and to let him heal us. He reminds us that our prayer at this point connects with the wound at the heart of the world. It is the Spirit 'groaning within us'.

In the final two chapters, John takes us to a place of inner healing and restoration through an encounter with Christ who is the only Word: this Word, Jesus, who is 'full of grace and truth', 'the way, the truth and the life', revealed and received in faith. The author then invites us to enter, through John's *Spiritual Canticle*, into the prayer of praise, with pure wonder at the workings of God in creation and in every human soul. Finally, the Epilogue opens up for us John's insights into God's fatherliness towards the Son and to all of creation, calling us to respond by living as children of the Father – welcoming people into our hearts as our brothers and sisters, and receiving the gift of God himself as his beloved sons and daughters.

Although John was born in the sixteenth century, we see from these pages that his teaching is remarkably relevant to us in our own rapidly changing world, with our many pressing concerns today. We can see this relevance from how the author presents the teaching of John on prayer, which the book does in a most enlightening way supported by a deft choice of John's writings. Iain Matthew's insights into the depth, beauty and subtlety of John's poetic works are both original and invaluable. They contain many of John's most profound teachings on prayer. Where relevant, the author directs us to the biographical background, to help us understand the origins of John's spiritual insights. Several times, for example, he reminds us of the saint's imprisonment in Toledo where much of his greatest poetry – 'The Dark Night', 'The Spiritual Canticle', 'How well I know the fount' and 'Romances' – was sharpened and refined on the anvil of suffering, misunderstanding and rejection.

We also learn from these pages that a major reason why John's teaching on prayer is able to address the concerns and needs of our troubled world is because of John's sensitivity to a *wound*. This 'wound' is an unease or dissatisfaction, an anxiety deep in the human heart which is always in search of peace and rest, meaning and deeper understanding. This need is a way of prayer. It is at the core of all human life, answering to the 'unquiet heart' of the Christian experience, the heart that is always restless until it rests in God.

We also find that John's teaching on prayer is eminently practical, keeping us in touch with the ordinary flesh-and-blood lives of people in search of God. We know that John has not always enjoyed a favourable press. His prose style has hardly helped his cause. But the author shows the saint's teaching to be extremely helpful and readable, even when exploring something as subtle as the Spirit's delicate action in the deepest recesses of the human heart.

John of the Cross: Seasons of Prayer presents, in a small format but with great spiritual depth, the riches of John's teachings on prayer, which will be of inestimable value to both the general reader and to all who are involved in guiding others along the way of prayer.

James McCaffrey, OCD
Editor of *Mount Carmel*

Abbreviations and References

1A / 2A / 3A	*The Ascent of Mount Carmel* (or *Ascent*) – Book 1 / 2 / 3
1DN / 2DN	*The Dark Night* (or *Night*) – Book 1 / 2
SC^A / SC^B	*The Spiritual Canticle* (or *Canticle*) – Redaction A / B
SC	Used where the poem's stanzas are the same in both Redactions
LF	*The Living Flame* (or *Flame*) – Redaction B used throughout
SLL	*Sayings of Light and Love* (or *Sayings*)
P	Poem
R	'Romances on the Trinity' (or 'Romances')
Lt	Letter

Italics are used for whole works or commentaries on the poem in question; quotation marks (without italics) for poems. Hence: *Canticle* and 'Canticle'.

The numbering of John's *Sayings*, Poems and Letters (which can vary between editions) corresponds to the readily available standard English edition, *The Collected Works of Saint John of the Cross* (Washington, DC: ICS Publications, 1991). The same applies to the Letters of Teresa: numbering as in *The Collected Letters of St. Teresa of Avila*, 2 vols. (Washington, DC: ICS Publications, 2001 & 2007). All translations in the current book, however, are my own.

Biographical Introduction

'His face used to radiate peace and joy – he never appeared depressed, nor vexed with himself or those under his authority; he always treated people gently.'[1] So a fellow friar describes St John of the Cross. This introduction taps the source of his inner joy.

Certainly such joy is not the fruit of mere absence of pain. John was born into a poor weaving family in barren Castile in 1542. His father, Gonzalo de Yepes, had been disinherited for marrying beneath him, and John's early years were marked by the affection and penury such a marriage involved. Gonzalo's early death left Catalina and the two surviving children, Francisco and John, destitute. The mother traipsed from one urban centre to another seeking work, finally settling in Medina del Campo, Castile's international trade centre. Happily, John was received into a school for the poor there – well prepared, then, to begin work in his later teens with the dying in a Medina hospital. After years tending the sick, begging for them in the bustling town, studying late at night for classes in the recently founded Jesuit College, John (now twenty-one) came to a mature decision to dedicate his life to God in the Carmelite Order.

His formation as a Carmelite took him to another European centre: the university town of Salamanca, the scene for John of several years of academic and community life, university controversy and cloistered regularity. But when he was all set for ordination, crisis ensued: perhaps it was the contrast between the relative comfort of his Salamanca days and his childhood encounter with life's open wounds that made John question his Carmelite life and nerved him to opt for a more severe – Carthusian – existence. He was decided when, in 1567, he met St Teresa of Avila: she recognised his spirit, told him of her plans to reform the Carmelite Order, and won him to the cause.

Duruelo, a hamlet in the Castilian wilderness: here John and three companions inaugurated the life of the Discalced Carmelite friars – intense prayer, simple pastoral care of the neighbouring villages, severe poverty. The reform quickly grew, and houses of formation were set up.

John, still a young man, rejoined Teresa in 1572: 'la Madre' had called for him to help her lead the convent of the Incarnation in Avila – some one hundred and eighty sisters were there, demoralised, poor with a poverty not of their choosing, fearful of talk of reform. John's tact and gentleness had a remarkable effect, and the community underwent a profound renewal.

But John's presence aggravated friars who did not share his spirit, and, in December of 1577, the antagonism which the whole reform business was creating was unleashed on this simple man. John was kidnapped, taken in secret across the Guadarrama mountains, to be incarcerated in a monastery in Toledo. So began nine months of solitary confinement, in a minute dungeon, deprived of light, adequate food, a change of clothes, in freezing cold turning in summer to stifling heat; the prisoner was allowed out weekly – to be flogged. With this went a kind of psychological torture and the threat of death; and, deep in his spirit, affliction even in his relationship with God.

Yet in this confinement, darkness and anguish, the belly of Jonah's sea-beast as he was to describe it, John discovered the presence of Christ his Beloved in a way that brought light, freedom and peace: 'the inner resurrection of the spirit' (2DN 6:1). It is this 'resurrection' that he sings in his poems, composed and written in prison – among them, 'The Spiritual Canticle'.

John was not only a mystic and poet; he was also eminently practical, as his captors discovered in mid-August 1578: in most dramatic fashion, during the night, John had escaped from the prison. Able to rejoin his brethren, John was sent to the relative safety of Andalusia. In the friaries in the south of Spain, John spent ten years – the solitude of the Sierra de Segura; the Inquisition-raided university town of Baeza; the poor monastery overlooking the luxuriant Moorish palace in Granada. Deep prayer and care of his brother and sister Carmelites was coupled with periods of literary activity and extensive travels as Vicar-Provincial. In an age marked by extremes of religious rigorism or indifference, John stood out for his personal care and ability to awaken faith.

Back in Castile, John was nominated to the priory in Segovia in 1588. Here began the last and perhaps blackest night for John – but one which his love for the Bridegroom turned to day. Conflict was brewing at the top: the then superior was pushing through policies which John considered injurious to the Order and unjust to individuals. At the same time John found himself the victim of a sinister libel campaign, spearheaded by one of his former subjects. The campaign intended to have John thrown out of the reform – the reform he had lived and nearly died for. In this setting, his words reveal their true mettle: 'Where there is no love, put love, and you will draw out love.'[2]

While this campaign was being waged, John was preparing to carry out his superiors' latest direction: he had been appointed to sail for Mexico. But the 'slight bout of fever'[3] which took him to Ubeda for treatment turned out to be erysipelas – a disgusting disease, rivalled only by the pain of the surgery and the aggression of the Prior who resented John's presence. Love, here, did draw out love: as John lay dying, the weeping Prior begged his forgiveness.

The scene is a cameo of that mixture of affection and aggression, joy and pain, that John had met throughout his life – in which he had learned to recognise 'the night' as the casket 'containing the hope of day' (cf. 2DN 9:8). He died as one coming home – home to the Bridegroom who had taught him how to live: 'At evening,' John had said, 'you will be examined in love. Learn to love, then, as God wishes' (SLL 60).

He died in the first moments of December 14, 1591, just as the bells were chiming midnight.

Chapter 1
Prayer as Presence

During these days, let your heart be taken up in wanting the Holy Spirit to come; and at Pentecost and after, be taken up in the Spirit's constant presence. Let this be so important to you that nothing else will matter to you or draw your attention; nothing painful, no unsettling memory. Throughout these days, even if others' behaviour at home is not as it should be, let it be, for love of the Holy Spirit. You owe it to your heart to give it this peace and stillness, since your heart is a place where the Spirit is pleased to dwell.[1]

This is a tender letter, measured to one woman's pain, leading her to new possibilities. It is also a characteristic letter, declaring what John habitually saw, and the way this led him to pray. What he saw was presence: 'the Spirit's constant presence'. His prayer was to welcome that presence. These opening pages are an invitation to pick up John's sense that presence is paramount, and to hear his lesson of welcome.

Nothing less will satisfy

'At recreation and other times he would usually sit on the floor among the friars; and seeing him do this, they would do the same.'[2] This testimony to John's behaviour in community depicts his soul: being there for the other, and opening the other by being there. He learned this in prayer. There he sits by the One who, laying aside his outer garment and dressing like a slave, has sat there first. The God of John's prayer is the one who is present, and whose openness opens us to him.

There could be other emphases. St Ignatius Loyola can sign off his letters, praying 'that we might feel his most holy will and entirely fulfil it'. His *Exercises* lead to a perception of that will and to a ready 'yes'. Such prayer is the prayer of Jesus who assents to the will of the Father.

John of the Cross typically begins his letters, 'Jesus be in your soul'. His wish for his correspondents is that Jesus should 'be in' them: that Christ and the person be intimately available to one another. His prayer is the prayer of Jesus who 'abides in' the love of the Father.

Ignatius and John say the same thing. Both were mystics, both were hearers and doers of the word. But there are nuances, and if Ignatius' life was 'a permanent "election"',[3] John's was a permanent reception – 'the Spirit's constant presence'.

Presence, or absence, is the issue. The core need

that is felt in night is the need of acceptance by, and connection with, the other. What most strips the person is *not dryness*, or confusion, or revulsion at oneself, but a sense of *rejection*, *alienation*: the loved one has gone (cf. 2DN 6:2; 7:7).

So the Jesus, who in *Ascent* makes of darkness a healing place, cries out: 'Why have you forsaken me?' (2A 7:11; Mt 27:46). Why are you not here? The key issue in the crucifixion is not asphyxiation or traumatic shock, but the presence, or absence, of the Father.

John's cry in Toledo is not, What must I do? but, Where have you gone? 'Where have you hidden, Beloved…?' The issue is the presence, or absence, of Christ.

The human face

The Spiritual Canticle reveals just this personal focus. If reading were limited to *The Ascent of Mount Carmel*, a powerful vision of prayer would emerge: a progressive opening to divine inflowing. *Canticle* is more lyrical, picturesque, ostensibly less useful. But it is essential to understanding John's message. *Canticle* discloses a face, where other writings might suggest just a system. What drives the author of *Ascent* in advocating detachment, faith, contemplative stillness, is his passion for the person of Christ.

So the first twelve stanzas, the bride's breathless

quest for the hidden spouse, focus the reader in only one direction. Where is he? (SC, stanza 1). If you see him, tell him I need him (2). I shall not stop until I find him (3). Tell me, have *you* seen him? (4). (Then, to the Beloved:) Please, no more messages – *you* be the messenger and the message! (6). Mere news of you is not enough (7). Let me see *you* – no one else will do (10). As John comments: 'Since she sees that nothing can cure her pain except the presence, the sight, of her Beloved', she abandons 'hope in any other remedy…' (SC[B] 6:2).

Canticle was a work in progress. Begun in Toledo, poem and commentary grew after escape as John's experience blossomed. The last stanza to be composed he located as stanza 11.[4] It declares superbly the focus of his longing:

Descubre tu presencia,	Unveil now your presence
y máteme tu vista y	and let the vision of your
* hermosura;*	beauty slay me.
mira que la dolencia	See how the pain
de amor, que no se cura	of love will only heal
sino con la presencia y	if you are here and let me
* la figura.*	see your face.

(SC[B], stanza 11)

This focus of *Canticle* is itself a lesson in prayer. The heart of prayer is the other person: a presence and a face, *presencia y figura*. Being with him is a value worthy of a person's life.

Heart presence

'Let this be so important to you that nothing else will matter to you...' The presence of which John speaks is heart presence, not mere geography. Neighbouring bodies may sandwich you on the underground, but there is no presence. You can be a hemisphere away from a friend, and still be close.

John means it when he says that the soul *lives where it loves* (cf. SC[A] 8:2).[5] The spirit is the person at her most mobile. Love makes one participate, for better or worse, in what is loved. This has its downside in lust and addiction, where yearning shapes one to the smallness of one's obsessions. But the power of love to 'make present' has its glory in God, where the love of Father and Son means that each lives in the other, and the Spirit-love uniting them makes them a single lover (cf. R 1-3). God's love creates the universe that it may join this circle of availability (cf. R 4).

John's 'let it be' – let go; put it *down*! – is an education in availability. He had been trained in this himself: prayer, spent in raw expectancy or in hushed attention; time tending the diseased or receiving a brother's despondency. Faith, not pet ideas, hope, not ambition, charity, not selective affections, had made John Godlike in his openness. Here, John and Ignatius join company. If the Carmelite call is to 'be with' Christ, such companionship demands surrender. Presence means not spatial proximity but hearts in tune.

So John can define union – two being together – as oneness of will (cf. 2A 5); and he has a Thérèse-like focus on the desire to 'please' God.[6] *Canticle* puts this desire in its own idiom. Stanza 17 echoes *The Dark Night* in its intensity: 'the experiences of the Beloved's *absence* which the soul suffers in this state of spiritual betrothal are a cause of great affliction. At times they are such that no pain can compare with them. The reason is that, since her love for God in this state is great and strong, great and strong is the torment of love in his absence' (SC[B] 17:1; cf. 2DN 11-13). So she invokes the 'south wind' – the Holy Spirit – who will dispel winter's chill, increase her love, and wake up the fragrance of virtue in the soul. But her main aim in doing this is 'that the Son of God, her Bridegroom, might rejoice and delight more in her, since for her the point of everything is to make her Beloved happy' (SC[B] 17:2; cf. 17:8).

'Being with' is heart presence; wanting what he wants; wanting to bring him joy.

Easter witness

Presence, as persons, in tune, is the issue. And that presence is a reality. This is John's primary gift to the Church, his testimony to the givenness of God.

When the Carmelite escaped from his dungeon, he took with him the tale of a God whose closeness took his breath away. His poems sing this gift of togetherness: 'resting her neck on the fair arms of the Beloved' (SC[B], stanza 22); 'my face resting on the Beloved' (DN, stanza 8); 'you wake in my heart / where secretly, alone, you dwell' (LF, stanza 4). Contemplation, a loving attention to God's loving light, is this togetherness, assent in harmony, two hearts trustingly laid bare.

The apex of John's experience shows just how vulnerable God wills to be. The workmanlike progress of *Ascent* leads to a discourse on 'understanding of naked truth' (2A 26). Here the author turns hushed, abashed: 'for you should know, beloved reader, that [this gift to the soul] is beyond any words' (2A 26:1). With awe he speaks of 'pure contemplation', the 'union' which is the journey's goal:

> a kind of touch of God upon the soul; so God himself is the one who is experienced and tasted there. And though this does not take place in an evident way, with clarity, as is the case in glory, yet this touch is so delicate a knowing and excellent a taste that it penetrates the core of the person's being [*sustancia del alma*]. (2A 26:5)

In this there is no danger of deception, since no counterfeit experience 'could enter the substance of the soul and renew it and set it alive with love, all in a single moment. This gift of naked knowledge of God does that' (2A 26:6).

Here the mystic testifies, at white heat, to the way God is. The word he offers to the Church is a witness to the all-available Christ. His is Easter prayer, an experience of the one who ascended 'to fill the whole universe with his presence' (Eph 4:10)[7] – he who, receiving 'from the Father the promise of the Holy Spirit, has poured out this which you see and hear' (Acts 2:33).

Companions in the night

Writing from a sun-blessed summit, John sees the world pervaded with light – 'the Spirit's constant presence'. That lets him read rightly the absence felt in the climb. His confidence is arresting: 'This dark night is an inflowing of God into the soul,…in which God is secretly teaching the soul and training her in perfect love' (2DN 5:1). What seemed to be darkness, absence, rejection, was really a mystery of presence: presence too close, too personal, too Godlike for the person's groundling senses to perceive. The Prologue to *Ascent-Night* sets out the diagnosis:

> It may happen that God will be carrying a person along a most favoured path of dark contemplation and dryness, and she feels she has lost her way… She seems to see it clear as

day: she is full of evils and sins; whereas in fact this comes from the light which God is giving her in that contemplative night. (A/DN Prol. 4-5)

Transformation takes place outside, beneath the stars, not in a familiar indoors with its fluorescent glare. Night means adjustment, sensitising the person to a gentler kind of closeness. 'Within this dark pain, this loving pain, the soul feels a certain inner strength and companionship, which accompanies and gives her strength…' (2DN 11:7).

The Pentecost letter with which we began ends on just this note, with encouragement not to fear the void: 'Live in faith and hope, even though it be in darkness, for in this darkness God is supporting the soul.'

Whose absence?

John's Easter witness to the closeness, even in night, of the all-pervading Christ, raises the question of just who it is that is absent. 'Lord my God! You are no stranger for the one who does not draw apart from you. How can they say that you are the one who is absent?' (SLL 50). The language of *Canticle* returns in the 'Shepherd' song (P 7), but this time in truer perspective. The one who suffers the other's absence, and longs for – dies for – her presence, is the man on the tree, his heart torn apart by love.[8]

Of Christ's presence there is no doubting. The mystic's awareness of this – God's givenness – clarifies the truth of every person: 'The centre of the soul is God' (LF 1:12). What is displayed is the communion hidden at the heart of each believer. So John's summit perspective lets him answer his *Canticle* question, 'Where...?' by saying, Don't you see: he is here. He is with you. He is in you. Welcome him.

> Soul, most beautiful among all creatures, you who so long to know the place of your Beloved, so as to seek him and become one with him! Now you are hearing the answer: you yourself are the room where he dwells... [He is] so close to you as to be within you... Desire him there, adore him there. (SC[B] 1:7-8)

In the terms of John's Pentecost letter: the Spirit is pressing in upon you; do not let worry stop you seeing that.

So, how to see it? How to come down to the floor where Christ is already kneeling, waiting? John's answer: 'seek him in faith and love' (SC[B] 1:11). This is the prayer of presence. One degree of love unites you with him at your centre (cf. LF 1:13). Believe, trust, love – and your presence to him becomes heart presence; you are together; you are with him. And his presence to you transforms.

Transformation

'Enter within your heart and work in the presence of the Bridegroom, who is always present, loving you well' (SLL 90). Enter and be with him, because the company you keep has power to change you.

Jean Vanier tells of the l'Arche community in Suyapa, Honduras. When Claudia came there, she 'was seven years old and had spent practically her whole life in a dismal, overcrowded asylum. Claudia was blind, fearful of relationships, filled with inner pain and anguish.' On arrival at the community, 'everything and everyone frightened her; she screamed day and night and smeared excrement on the walls.' But the companionship of people who loved her brought change. It was 'the gentle presence of Nadine and the others in Suyapa that gradually weakened Claudia's great walls of defence. Little by little, she began to trust that she was not bad, but capable of loving and being loved.'[9]

'Only being loved is being saved.'[10] Being with the one who loves is the road to healing. The simplicity of John's prayer, an attention in love to the one who is loving you, is a supremely 'happening' place. It holds out the possibility of transformation: that in being with him, we would be made like him.

Commenting on the line, 'There you will show me' (SC[A], stanza 37), *Canticle* attests to this power of God's love to open new possibilities in the heart:

> In this transformation, God communicates himself to the soul: he shows her love, love that is total, generous and pure; love in which he communicates the whole of himself to her, *most* lovingly, transforming her in himself… So this really is 'showing her how' to love – [like a craftsman] putting the instrument in her hands, telling her how to use it, and using it along with her. (SC[A] 37:3)

Prayer here is divine apprenticeship, in which God's tenderness makes the soul, too, an expert in loving – *maestra de amar*:

> So it is that the soul has been not only instructed in love; she has become an expert in loving, united with the expert himself, and, as a result, she has found fulfilment; fulfilment will be hers only when she comes to love like this. (SC[A] 37:3)

The prayer of the poor

Utilitarian ethics and a sensationalist culture have little room for those who find it hard to communicate; little esteem 'for anyone who, like the unborn or the dying, is a weak element in the social structure, or for anyone who appears completely at the mercy of others and radically dependent on them, and can only communicate through the silent language of a profound sharing of affection.'[11]

In this light, the prayer welcoming 'the Spirit's constant presence' is no esoteric affair. Like Mary standing by her Son when he was at others' mercy, the prayer of presence sets the believer alongside those who cannot compete. It takes one to a spacious, night-time place, where the veins of the world's suffering meet; the home of the incompetent and defenceless, who 'can only communicate through the silent language of a profound sharing of affection'. For John, being with Christ in that still place is a priority – 'so important to you that nothing else [should] matter to you or draw your attention'. A world in pain is waiting there.

As the postscript to another letter puts it:

Our greatest need is to be silent before this great God, silent in spirit and with the tongue; for his only language, the one he hears, is the silent language of love.[12]

Chapter 2
Praying from Our Need

And I am feeling very well, glory be to God, and doing fine. The openness of the wilderness really does soul and body good – though my soul is in great poverty. The Lord must want it to have its own spiritual desert. Well and good, so long as that is what pleases him. His Majesty already knows what we are when left to ourselves. (Lt 28)

This is John of the Cross writing to his friend Ana de Peñalosa in August 1591, a month before his final sickness began to overpower him. It is a bewildering time. John's moral authority had once led him to positions of influence and respect in his Order. Now, abruptly, he has found himself on the sidelines, a focus of controversy, victim of a campaign to have his name disgraced. 'Just being his friend was a crime.'[1]

John is writing from La Peñuela, an isolated monastery in the foothills of the Sierra Morena in the south of Spain, far away from the responsibilities and politics of Castile. The stillness is a mirror of his own spirit: a still point in a jostling, jealous world.

In the midst of all this, John is in desert surroundings, *el desierto*. He is pleased to be there. It 'does soul and body good'. He relishes the solitude, openness, *anchura*, room to breathe. Apparently, it was during this time that he re-edited his most personal and intense writing, *The Living Flame*. The desert lets him connect with what is truest in him.

It is also a place where he knows his poverty: 'my soul is in great poverty' – a desert of the spirit, where he is not simply in command, where things do not just work for him. That, too, can be a good place. It spells surrender to God's plan, not the pushing of his own.

John encourages us to go there. The place of poverty within us is the threshold at which Christ stands. Our need is a way of prayer.

John, the voice of fragility

'People do not know how rightly to rejoice, nor how rightly to mourn, for they do not know the distance between good and evil' (SLL 63). In the face of the world's pain, John's writing can seem rather private, too slow-moving to keep up with human need. In fact, the vaster the pain, the more vital John's word. When the need is so far-reaching, superficial solutions will not do. John is one who *has* travelled the distance, from darkness to light; he has been led to the places within him which border on good and evil. Knowing that distance, his word goes to the root causes and can lead us, not to superficial adjustment, but to a gospel mourning and a genuine joy.

Given the quality of John's testimony, it is all the more illuminating, then, to see where his word originates. The events in his story are worth recalling once more, to highlight this one fact: that John's word issues from a history of weakness.

One witness was later to speak of the striking conjunction in John of strength, commitment, on the one hand, and gentleness, mildness, on the other.[2] His life had fired him to just that temper. The death of his father and brother when John was an infant; his displacement as a child as the family looked for a living; John's work as a teenager with people dying of syphilis; a crisis in direction at the time of his ordination, through which Teresa helped to guide him – these were so many events emptying his spirit, carving out a nothingness, an expectancy, for the divine.

The honing of his spirit came to a head in circumstances where his weakness was extreme: months of imprisonment in Toledo for his part in the Teresian reform. Transferred to a tiny, dark dungeon, where hunger, squalor and isolation could set to work, John was pushed there beyond thresholds he had never had to cross before, into unfamiliar regions where his emotional and physical weakness would have made him very vulnerable.

And it is precisely here that John began composing his most personal poetry, from which his writings derive.

That, then, is a first indication for us from John about prayer: the place within us where not everything is all right, where the wound that is in you aches. John says: Go there.

The wound is the place where God dwells

Go to that place of need, because that is a threshold at which Christ stands; our need is an evidence of God. This is a second lesson from John on prayer.

It is said that physical hunger passes through three phases.[3] You stop eating and you need food and that is hard to cope with. But as time passes, the body settles into a rhythm, feeding on its fat reserves. The point comes, though, when these reserves run out and the body begins to feed on its own substance. Then hunger turns into a desperate craving, all the person's instinct to preserve their life invested now in this, the body's cry.

In our life of faith, too, there are levels and phases. Perhaps we are in that second phase: what once was powerful and compelling has settled down, a steady jog, feeding on reserves. But if we were taken further, to that third level of hunger, what would we find? That was the place John reached, and from which his prison poem, 'The Spiritual Canticle', begins – a word that issues from the substance of his spirit, the heart's cry, craving for life:

¿Adonde te escondiste,	Where have you hidden,
Amado, y me dejaste	Beloved, and left me
con gemido?	groaning?
Como el ciervo huiste,	You fled like the stag,
habiéndome herido;	having wounded me;
salí tras ti clamando,	I went out in search of
y eras ido.	you, and you were gone.
	(SC, stanza 1)

This stanza, expertly crafted and couched in Song of Songs language, is the cry of John's spirit. He has experienced a wound within him. He calls out from there. Calls out for what?

At this point in his life, with dungeon walls and lice for company, John had many needs. He lacked light, warmth, food, clean clothing, medicine for his wounds; he might have been helped by reassurance that he had not made a mistake, that his life's endeavour would be fruitful, that his friends still believed in him. All these protective layers were being stripped off him. But when he is exposed in this way, what he calls out for is none of these: God, give me light, clothing, safety, friendship, a welcome, a future. What he cries for is '*you*': a person, Another; Christ. 'Where have *you* hidden, Beloved...?' It

39

is as if the removal of all those layers laid bare a deeper wound, the need which John is: it reveals John as a need for God.

John confirms that for us, too, there is a third level of hunger, where our reality, the 'substance' of the soul, is crying out for God. To be taken there is an immense blessing. Our need is the measure of our dignity, the reverse image of our greatness. When the person is empty and cleansed, 'the thirst and hunger and the spirit's feeling of longing is more than can be borne... The capacity of these caverns is deep, for that which can fill them is deep, infinite; and that is God. So in a sense their capacity will be infinite, and so their thirst infinite, their hunger too is deep and infinite, their sense of undoing and pain is an infinite death... since the soul is in a sense ready to receive what will fill her' (LF 3:18.22).

It is natural to flee from the place where that hunger throbs. Still John encourages us to go there. It is what beckons the divine. It is the threshold at which Christ stands. We hunger for him because he has touched us; we want him because he wants us. The wound is the print of the pledge upon us, the pledge of the Spirit who holds us from the abyss. John comments on his poem: we 'have our feeling of longing, the sense of God's absence' precisely there, 'within our heart, where we have the pledge' (SC[A] 1:6).

Two pointers, then, about prayer from John of

the Cross: go to the fragile place; it is Christ who is waiting there.

Open spaces and the terror of the night

Thirdly, much of John's system is really about this: trying to get us there, to the place of our need; to get us to go there, and stay there. The desert can be scary. The spirit suffers from a natural agoraphobia. The night is disconcerting: safer back in the house, with the glow of party lights and small talk.

In *The Ascent of Mount Carmel*, John expends his energy encouraging us not to lose our nerve or settle for a cheap alternative. When the wound that is in you begins to ache, or the anaesthetic in you starts wearing off, do not grasp for compensation. Stay there. Show yourself you can stand there. Do not be a slave to the fear of not being anaesthetised. Risk stepping into that open space where you need God. 'Step free of your longings and you will find what your heart really longs for…' (SLL 15).

In the books of *The Dark Night*, John is talking to people who are being taken there. John's *nada* is mystical, a nothingness into which he himself was led, far beyond the regions of his expertise. In that aching, open, darkened place, the temptation is to read the openness as emptiness, and to panic. John says, rather: Stay there; let God work there;

say 'yes' to the God who is feeding you precisely there.

> The person was wearing this white garment of faith as she went out in this dark night. She wore it as she journeyed…in inner darkness and oppression, when her mind was giving her no relief: no light from above, since heaven seemed closed and God seemed hidden; no light from below, since her teachers were failing to meet her need. On this journey, she persevered, bearing it with constancy, passing through these difficulties without giving up or giving up on her Beloved. (2DN 21:5)

In probing our neediness, the books of *Night* find signs of God's action. When prayer is no longer functioning the way it once did, but has become tasteless, and the person feels disorientated, reaching out for a God who is no longer showing up: John sees that reaching, that anxiety for God, as a sign of God's action (cf. 1DN 9).

Again, when a person experiences their weakness as never before, feels that they do not fit, that they are unacceptable, all the rubbish in them now floating like jetsam to the surface: John sees that as a fruit of God tenderly, hiddenly, drawing near; a fruit of God's action (cf. 2DN 7).

To the question, Where is God?, John is answering by pointing to where we feel most needy.

The wound at the heart of the world

When in *Night* John seeks words for the wound that is in him, it is the cries of Israel that surface: the Psalms, Lamentations, Job – individuals who voiced the pain of their people. The wound to which John descends, 'Where have you hidden...?', connects with the pain of the world. It is as if, deep beneath the surface where we perform and survive, there lay a reservoir of weakness where we are all one. In his solitary confinement John was accessing a universal cry.

The word John uses in the first stanza of his 'Canticle' conveys this: *gemido* – 'Where have you hidden, / Beloved, and left me *groaning*?' In the Prologue to his commentary, John speaks of his verses as an echo of the Spirit who pleads for us with a cry too deep for words: *gemidos inefables* (SC[B] Prol. 1). From the wound within him rises the cry of the Spirit. It is a cry which gives voice to the longing of the whole of creation to be set free:

> the creation itself will be set free from its bondage to decay and obtain the glorious liberty of the children of God. We know that the whole of creation has been groaning in travail together until now; and not only the creation, but we ourselves, who have the first fruits of the Spirit, groan inwardly as we wait for adoption... (Rm 8:21-23)

In another prison poem, 'Romances on the Trinity' (also known as the 'Ballads'), John pictures humanity longing for the coming of the Bridegroom, begging 'with tears and cries' (*con lágrimas y gemidos*) for the 'companionship' of the Son of God (cf. R 5).[4] Individuals are pictured voicing the Advent prayer of the Church. So it is that those who are taken by God to the place of hunger within them stand there on behalf of their people. They give voice to the cry, the need, of the universe. Such purified prayer is a source of healing: 'a little of this pure love is more precious to God and for the soul, and of more benefit to the Church' – and so, to the world – '...than all those other works put together' (SC[B] 29:2).

Christ is the guarantee of this – the wounded Christ, a brother in our need. So John puts at the head of his treatise *Ascent-Night* the picture of Jesus reconciling humanity, restoring the universe, as he enters the black hole where God seems not to be. John knows an annihilated Christ who was 'compelled to cry out: *My God! My God! Why have you forsaken me?*' And John continues: 'This was the most extreme forsakenness he had felt in his life. And by it he did his greatest work, greater than any he had done in his life... That is, he reconciled and united the human race with God...' (2A 7:11; cf. Mt 27:46).

The journey to our poverty, then, is not a private affair; the healing of the world is at stake.

Let your need be your prayer

This, then, is one of the seasons of prayer in John of the Cross. We have been led by him to Cana: the family wedding where the wine runs out. Mary sees the anxiety, and has a quiet word with her Son just pointing out what she has noticed.

This is a scene with cosmic scope: the wedding of the Lamb, espousing humanity, a humanity in peril. The mother of Jesus perceives what is lacking, and names it, without dictating a solution: 'They have no wine' (Jn 2:3). Hers is a prayer of need; her perception of need is a prayer. She takes it, holds it, allows it to ache before him. And that precipitates glory. He 'manifested his glory; and his disciples believed in him' (Jn 2:11).

This, then, is a way of prayer: to feel our way to the wound that is in us, to the place of our need. Go there, take it, name it; hold it before Christ.

To feel our way to the wounds of the world, to those people or situations in dire need of healing. Go there, take them, name them, and hold them before him.

Go there, not to dictate to Christ what the answer should be or what he should do about it; but to hold the wound before him.

'They have no wine.' John of the Cross sees wisdom here. A love which does not spell out 'what it needs or wants, but holds out its need so that the Beloved might do what pleases him' is especially powerful:

> And this for three reasons: firstly, because the Lord knows what is best for us, better than we do; second, because the Beloved's compassion is more deeply moved when he sees the need and the surrender of the one who loves him; third, because the soul is less vulnerable to her self-love and possessiveness when she holds out the need before him than when she spells out her own view of what it is she needs. (SC[B] 2:8)

This, then, is a way of prayer in John of the Cross: to go to the place of our need, and to hold that before God. 'We have no wine' – a service to the world, a prayer that precipitates glory.

Chapter 3
Prayer:
Anointing the Mind

In teaching prayer, John of the Cross has led us to the place of our need, and has shared his wonder at God's gift there. In the prayer of need, the encounter, God's gift of himself to the human spirit, is a place of healing and restoration. John expresses this in many ways. What follows is an attempt to reach one expression of this healing encounter. It focuses on the second book of *The Ascent of Mount Carmel*. There, John gives us this invitation: Let light bathe your mind.

Beyond maintenance

The Ascent of Mount Carmel is methodical, deliberately repetitive. It is like Ravel's *Bolero*, throbbing on till its rhythm gets inside us and we cannot but consent to its rightness. Book 1 says loudly: We need to be set free. Books 2 and 3 set out the path to freedom. They are a kind of surgery of the spirit, opening up the inner self in order to anoint it.

To help the diagnosis, John looks at the self as three powers: understanding, memory, and will. Not three 'things', like three bodily organs, but the whole person understanding and knowing, conscious and recalling, loving and choosing.[1] Static as it may seem, John's analysis deserves a hearing, because it lets him offer genuinely good news. Through it he proposes nothing less than a transformation of the self. He digs down and cracks open the soil so that the water can really seep in, not just run off the surface. He analyses the inner self because the self is to be healed:

> What we have to do, then, is to treat of how the three powers of the soul (understanding, memory and will) are led into this spiritual night, in and through which union with God can take place... We shall go on to look at how the understanding has to be *completed* in the darkness of faith; the memory, in the emptiness of hope; and how the will, too, is *to be made whole* when she is stripped of every craving, carrying nothing in her journey to God. (2A 6:1)[2]

Faith making the mind complete; hope restoring the memory; love making the will, the heart, whole. John is responding here to a gospel call: *metánoia*, conversion, a refashioning of the *nous*. Let your spirit be overturned. Change your way of thinking. Allow an alternative light to anoint your mind.

In *Ascent*, John painstakingly confronts the mind's resistance and opens it to that other light. This sense of prayer, as accepting a healing light, is what we want to get hold of in these pages.[3]

The human mind – a place of welcome

Faith, hope and love 'walk as one' (2A 24:8). What John says of faith, then, can cover the whole human response to God. And among John's subdivisions, it is faith and the understanding that receive the most incisive treatment in the books of the *Ascent*.

Faith has a beautiful spaciousness to it. It is like sunlight blessing a spring day. The mind has a tender receptivity to it, like eyes opening to the light. For all its sturdiness, what John is driving home in *Ascent* serves a prayer that is childlike and surprised.

In our technocratic age, the mind might appear more like the great achiever: that by which humanity unlocks and controls the cosmos. Knowledge is power, a key to dominance. The mind makes a person king and lets him ravage the earth.

John's view of mind, *entendimiento*, is different. The mind is indeed an agent of knowledge. (John's expertise in philosophy, verse, and the realities of water transportation prove his readiness to crack a problem by hard work.) The mind does, then, achieve and attain. But for John, the mind's deepest characteristic is its ability to receive, to welcome, to let in.[4] Like receptive paper welcoming print, the mind is the person capable of being formed, shaped, attuned to what is seen.

The eye is vulnerable; it can smart if unprotected. George Herbert, in his poem 'Virtue', catches this beautifully: 'Sweet rose, whose hue angry and brave / Bids the rash gazer wipe his eye…' Beauty does not simply sit there: it radiates. It pumps out light. Make sure you really want to look at it: because if you cast your eye at it unguarded, its flare will be too much for you!

The soul's eyes are the mind (cf. 2A 23:2). Understanding is seeing. To understand is indeed to work, to examine; but it is, still more, to receive a light.

Understanding is hearing. The mind is me, open to the word; most itself when it is able to listen. Listening, we attain to what is deepest. Ancient Heraclitus spoke of contemplation as 'listening to the essence of things'.[5] The mind's health depends not on how many ideas it has acquired, but on how free it is to hear.

How free am I to hear what you are saying? How free am I to hear what you are not saying? How willing is my mind to let itself be bathed in another's light? To grow in understanding, the person must do that difficult thing: 'retain a mind bigger than its own ideas'.[6]

If the mind is more deeply receiver than achiever, the key question is: What have I been receiving? To what am I giving authority over my mind? What issues have I let print themselves upon me? What worries or goals am I allowing to shape me?

As John leads us forward in *The Ascent of Mount Carmel*, this is his continual question: What, who, is shaping your mind? Who has authority over it?

And his proposal for healing is this: Let your mind be shaped in faith. Set up in your mind the candle of faith (cf. 2A 16:15). Let God's word print itself upon you. Let the gospel light anoint your mind (cf. 2A 3:3).

How far does your welcome go?

When John speaks of faith, two questions arise. One is the content of faith: what light must anoint us? We shall come to that. The other is about our openness to that light: how deeply are we receiving? Faith operates at our place of deepest welcome. Throughout Book 2 of *Ascent* John is saying: Don't close down too early.

Though wonder takes place in a moment, it dislikes rush. In a world in search of hard evidence, rapid sensations and super-heroes, it is hard to welcome a gentler light. John's call for detachment is meant to retrain our powers of seeing and hearing. He opposes what weighs us down (*embarazar*), what impedes (*impedir*), what overfeeds (*cebar*) (2A 16:6; 15:3). He warns us off the fast food which makes manna hard to taste (cf. 1A 5:3).

What opposes the mind's receptivity is not endeavour or inventiveness. What opposes it is self: the dominance of my own criteria as I look out on the world. My craving to be acknowledged, recognised, approved, central – this crosses my eyes and tunnels my vision. Ingrown love fogs out the mind and the sun cannot get through:

> The mind is not able to let God's wisdom enlighten it, just as the sun's light cannot get through on a miserable day; nor can the will embrace God in itself in pure love, as a mirror which is misted over cannot reflect clearly the person's face; still less can the memory, which our confusing cravings have clouded over, receive serenely the form of God's image... (1A 8:2)

What John seeks to do in Book 2 of *Ascent* is take us further: You are worth more than that; you are meant for a love greater than that. Not this, not that, not that – go forward, only, in faith.

This receptive place, where faith is at home, John calls 'spirit'. The spirit is the person at the level of widest welcome. No narrower opening can hold all that faith wants to say. So, go beyond the stickiness of sense – reliance on what you can feel or finger over with your thoughts; and open to the spaciousness of spirit – where you can receive the whole of what is given, without slicing it up as soon as it arrives.

> The eyes of the soul must withdraw from all these things that she can get hold of...and set them on what she does not see, on what sense does not control: set them on spirit...which is what carries her to union in faith. (2A 16:12)[7]

So John's word in Book 2 of *Ascent* answers the question: How deeply are you willing to receive – how open can you be? His answer: Go beyond fluorescent light and fashion, and enter 'the abyss of faith' (2A 18:2), the region of reception, where one looks and sees.

'In him all things hold together...'

It must be hard for a mind to hold together in darkness and isolation. The mind could succumb. Terry Waite, in his struggle to keep a grip during years of solitary confinement in Beirut, knew he had to do *something*. He kept himself in place by telling over in his mind his life story.[8]

In the isolation of his Toledo prison, John, too, was perched on the thin ledge of his own mind. He had to do something. What he did is best expressed in his poetry. In the darkness of his dungeon, John let his mind be painted with light.

Each of the Toledo poems – 'Canticle', 'Fountain', 'Romances' – communicates that light. 'Canticle' is most colourful, but most elusive. The light-source there is a 'Beloved', central to John's existence but not defined. Nonetheless, the other prison poems give the Beloved a name.

'I *know well* the fountain, rushing and flowing, *though it be night*' (P 8:7). By faith, despite darkness, John knows. Into night he wills a different horizon: an overflowing source hidden in 'this living bread to give us life' (P 8:9): Christ, present in Eucharist and Church.

The 'Romance' on the Psalm 'By the rivers of Babylon' (P 10; cf. Ps 136/137) marries John's sorrow to Israel's pain in exile. But whereas the Psalmist concludes by calling for his captors' children to be dashed against the rock, John ends by taking refuge in the rock. With God's little ones, he draws near to 'the rock who [is] Christ'.

The 'Romances on the Trinity' – on the Prologue to the Fourth Gospel – are John's *lectio divina* of salvation history. The poet was suffering exclusion and repression, but his verses balance all history on a mystery of infinite welcome: the love of Father for Son, of Son for Father, love which is Spirit, and which shares joy in creating the world (R 1-4). Humanity is created for a love unbearably beyond it (R 5-6) but made accessible in the coming of the Son in flesh (R 7). The drama comes home in Mary, at Nazareth and Bethlehem

(R 8-9) as she consents to welcome 'God in the cradle' (R 9).

Humanity finds God's joy, the baby cries our tears – an exchange of wedding gifts which gives the Church her dignity but seals the child's fate. Amid the festivities, Mary alone seems to grasp the issues. The poem ends with her gazing in wonder – *en pasmo* – at what is taking place. She is taking it in, receiving it, allowing it to shape her spirit. Her posture was a pattern for John himself: letting light from the human Christ paint the walls of his mind.

Jesus, the light of faith

Eucharist-Christ, rock-Christ, infant-Christ: when John had to do something to keep his mind together, what he did was rest his eyes on the Son-made-human. The light which must anoint is Christ.

Saying this, two points follow. For John, Christ is the place of prayer. Second, Christ alone does not betray the freedom of the listening mind. Only he can fill all of faith's expectancy.

Throughout Book 2 of *Ascent*, John tries to keep the gates of our minds open. The fashionable and impressive, the lure of insight and experience, all promote themselves and say: You can shut the gates now; I'm inside. John's chapters keep announcing: That is very nice, but it is not enough; keep the gates open.

Open for what? What *is* enough? The answer comes in Chapter 22. There the frustrated reader is asking: Why does God give extraordinary experiences at all, if we are not meant to hold them? Indeed, why is the Bible so full of supernatural communications, if we should not seek them now? If you, John, keep saying: Drop it, and go forward in faith, then what is this 'faith' which merits the loss of everything else?

John's answer is: Christ. The Word in flesh. God become human.

He is all-sufficient and all-accessible. No other light is relevant outside of him. 'In giving us, as he did, his Son, his only Word,...[the Father] has spoken it *all* to us, once and for all' (2A 22:3).

God has no other word, not that God is exhausted, but because Christ is God's entire mind, unceasingly laid bare. 'God is as it were speechless: he has no more to say, because what he once said piecemeal through the prophets, he has now said totally in him, giving us the All, who is his Son' (2A 22:4).

Christ is sufficient, because he reaches all of us, the whole of us. There is no corner too lost or shadowy for him to find and claim. He comes *humanado*, 'humaned', 'Christ-man' (2A 22:6.7). John's Christ is all God is, in all we are: 'God in the feeding-trough' (R 9); 'this great God of ours, humiliated and crucified' (Lt 25). His answer meets us even when we are functioning badly and cannot cope. 'If you want me to answer you with some word of comfort, look at my Son, subject to me and subjected out of love for me, and afflicted, and you will see how many words he answers you' (2A 22:6).

Christ is sufficient, because the Word spoken once in flesh is risen and eternally valid. The Father holds him out to us as given. His energy is pressing ceaselessly upon the doors of the soul: 'He is my total message, my answer, my entire vision and revelation. This I have already spoken to you, answered, manifested, revealed, in giving him to you as brother, companion, master, ransom and reward' (2A 22:5).

Keep the mind open, receptive, listening, tuned to faith. Faith alone is wide enough to receive union with God (cf. 2A 9:1). Now this faith has a face and a name. 'Listen to him, for I now have no more faith to reveal' (2A 22:5). Only Christ will not short-change the mind's deepest welcome.

Jesus, the light of prayer

If, for John, Christ is the experience which never needs renouncing, he is the way of prayer.

That is so from the beginning. Book 1 of *Ascent* portrays the mesmerising power which our cravings can exercise. Chapter 13 suggests an initial remedy. It calls us bravely to let go of what is too small for our dignity: 'Endeavour to be inclined, not to... but to...' (1A 13:6). Yet this demanding invitation is rooted in love and presence: 'First of all, keep in yourself a longing to imitate *Christ* in all things, letting your life take on the form of his. To do this, you need to gaze at his life [*considerar*], so as to know how to imitate him and respond in all things as he would' (1A 13:3).

John favours, here, the prayer which walks around the gospel, has Jesus as companion, has his life as our living space. Get to know him, and you may find yourself living like him. Get to know him, but as 'brother and companion' (cf. 2A 22:5); seek him as spouse. Hold and handle the mysteries of Christ, he advises early in *Canticle*; turn them over in your heart, so that love might lay bare what faith encloses: 'your Bridegroom' (SC[B] 1:11). While John speaks of imitation, his longing is for presence. The Father is saying: 'Set your eyes only on [Christ], for in him I have said it all to you, revealed it all, and in him you will find more even than you ask for or desire' (2A 22:5).

If John points us, then, to the gospel word as the place of presence and healing, he is not enclosing us in a narrow space. Rather, he is asking us to stand where the Son of God can unleash his light. Faith means to harness the mind's whole receptivity and lay that bare to the impress of Christ.

So as the relationship grows, friendship will involve more of us. What once needed plenty of talk may become total, loving, peaceful and still (cf. 2A 14:2). 'It is like someone with their eyes open: just by keeping their eyes open, receptive, light comes to them' (2A 15:2). Contemplation is gospel light, but now unrefracted; the risen Christ coming whole, and making the person whole: 'the soul, now simple and pure, is transformed in Wisdom, simple and pure, who is the Son of God' (2A 15:4). Naked truth, white light, is Christ fulfilling his Last Supper promise: 'I will love... and reveal myself' (2A 26:10; cf. Jn 14:21).

John invites us, then, bravely to surrender to an all-embracing presence. In contrast with our insights and inspirations, what 'the Spirit communicates in faith...is as different in quality as purest gold to base metal; and in quantity, as the sea is greater than a drop of water. For in that other way, wisdom concerning one or two or three truths...is communicated to the soul; but in this way, there is communicated to her all the Wisdom of God in a total way, which is the Son of God, who is communicated to the soul in faith' (2A 29:6).

To repeat the question: What have I been receiving – to what have I given authority over my mind? The gospel does not restrict. Other lights restrict. John asks us not to fear keeping the gates wide open. Christ will not abuse that trust. Let him anoint your mind.

Chapter 4
A Song of Praise

✠

'Brother Francisco, what is the nature of God?'
'God is what He wants to be.'

So ran a conversation between John of the Cross and a brother in his community in Granada.[1] John loved Francisco's answer. It told of a God who is greater than we are, whose love is unearned, and whose coming causes wonder. Let us catch some of that wonder in these pages.

A vocation to praise

In speaking of amazement at the mystery of God, we are coming close to John's centre. We have seen a first movement in John's prayer: going to the place where we are poor, needy. But there is a movement more characteristic of John himself: a movement of wonder and praise.

We shall focus on *The Spiritual Canticle*. Here the author is, precisely, 'saying and singing the greatness of his Beloved' (SC[B] 14-15:2), released by Christ to 'love and desire and praise and thank and revere and cherish and call on God, all with the fragrance of love' (SC[B] 25:5).

You cannot just *decide* to write brilliant poetry. John's verses are *gifted* language – masterfully crafted, but fundamentally *received*. His stanzas are 'the sayings of love in mystical understanding' (SC[B] Prol. 1). They are born of his experience of God. A response, then, to a gift.

John's great poems – 'Canticle', 'Flame', 'Night', 'Fountain' – are eucharistic. They tell the story of God's deeds in John's life. John has come to know God as this: one who has loved him, transformed him as fire transforms, beckoned him into the night, and filled him with living water. In different ways, these poems are saying: You, my God, are this; you have been this to me; you are this for us; thank you.

By bearing witness in this way, John is fulfilling the vocation of all creation. Commenting on the lines from his 'Canticle' poem (SC[B], stanza 15), *la música callada, / la soledad sonora* ('hushed music, / resounding solitude'), John declares that meek creation is in fact exploding with praise, loudly 'testifying to the reality of God'. Each work of God is proclaiming God's greatness in accord with what it has received, 'giving voice to that which in her is God' (SC[B] 14-15:27.25).

That might sum up the mystic's mission in the Church. Creation's mouthpiece, she gives voice to that which in her is God. John, too, does that: declares the God he has come to know.

To hear this witness is itself an education in

prayer. Children can survive with scanty rations and hand-me-down clothing. But for a child to know joy, something more is needed. They must be treasured, nurtured in love. So with our prayer journey. Advice on what to do when we sit or kneel is important. But over and above any *how*, there is the horizon that makes the how worthwhile and true.

We know that John gives helpful advice on prayer. Prayer is a journey – a hill climb, or a flight by night – and he expertly offers provisions, direction. But prior to the how and the what, John's gift is a light cast throughout: You, Father, are this; you have been this to me; you are this for them.

That light – of praise to God – is John's fundamental gift.

That there is a Word

Revelation is a motive for wonder: not only what the Word declares, but the fact that there is a Word at all; that God has broken the skin of silence sealing off our world, and dialogue has begun.[2] John can help us retrieve this primordial amazement. He does so, because he takes the silence seriously. His praise has been tested by the barrenness of life.

Nowadays, we rightly expect information. 'The 7.44 from Bournemouth is running approximately

42 minutes late.' Delay is fair enough, but we do want to be told.

However, where persons are concerned, we cannot demand disclosure. You cannot force a child to like you. You cannot require another to love you, to let you into the inner regions of their heart.

Where God is concerned, all the more is this the case: the living God, who cannot be reduced to just one more element, even the mightiest, in my universe; who is not simply at my disposal; who cannot be constrained. That this God should open up to us is not automatic. John of the Cross treasured this divine otherness:

> You do very well to seek him always as hidden. You honour God greatly and indeed come close to him when you hold him to be nobler and deeper than anything you can attain. So…do not be like many heartless people who have a low opinion of God: they think that when they cannot understand him or sense or feel him, he is further away – when the truth is more the opposite: it is when they understand him less clearly, that they are coming closer to him. (SC[B] 1:12)

John's praise was smelted in this furnace of God's otherness. Teresa read John's Toledo imprisonment in that way: it confronted her with a God whose ways seemed strange. How can he?, she asks (with a typical feel for hygiene and for the friar's diminutive stature):

> I keep thinking about what they have done to Fray Juan de la Cruz. I can't understand how God can allow such things. Even you [Padre Gracián] don't know the whole story. He was in that prison for a whole nine months – he could scarcely fit, tiny as he is. No change of clothes for all that time, though he was on the point of death.[3]

'How can God allow such things?' John's experience there – as with any contradictory suffering – was a confrontation with a different kind of God, one who outstrips the boundaries of my mind.

Another letter of Teresa's takes things further: 'Awesome is the way God treats his friends – that is no insult, since he treated his Son the same way.'[4] What looked godless was in fact a gift of love, 'God treating his friends'. John describes a night-like obscurity that can submerge the spirit, where one's relationship with God feels cruelly in the balance. Yet he is convinced that this felt dissonance – the difference between narrow 'us' and a God who is infinitely spacious – is caused by the divine approach, not by divine anger or absence.[5] Night, for John, is an experience of God's love – but the love of the living God, awesome, mysterious, the holy God who cannot be constrained.

John's writing was born there. His prison song begins: Where are you?... you have gone. As 'Canticle' progresses, there is no permission to settle for something cheaper. John stays there, tasting his poverty, experiencing a God who cannot be mastered or bought:

¡Ay, quién podrá sanarme!	Who is there to heal me?
Acaba de entregarte ya de vero;	Give yourself now, fully and forever!
no quieras enviarme	I beg you now to send me
de hoy más ya mensaj- ero,	no more of these your messengers;
que no saben decirme lo que quiero.	they cannot speak the word I long to hear.

(SC, stanza 6)

'O God, your way is holy. What God is great as our God?' Night, the taste of God's silence, schools the soul in 'respect and courtesy'. Of God himself, John says, 'nothing could be said that would be like him.'[6]

John's God is not in the phone book, and there is no earthly reason why he should disclose himself.

A world addressed

So here, wonder begins. Though nothing in us could lay claim to this, and no earthly reason could demand it, yet God – the living, awesome God – chooses, in his love, to communicate himself, to us. We live in an addressed world.

To love is to reveal; to risk disclosing the self.[7] God, loving us, is taking that risk. John of the Cross helps us to be amazed at this.

So in the course of 'The Spiritual Canticle', after twelve stanzas of longing, asking, and anguish, at last, for a brief moment, ever so slightly, the Beloved draws back the veil on who he, God, is. John's eyes meet other eyes, those he bore sketched deep within his heart (cf. SC^B, stanza 12); and the sight, like lightning splitting the night, overwhelms him: 'Take them away,' the poet cries (SC^B, stanza 13). But from that moment's encounter, a litany of praise – 'saying and singing the greatness of her Beloved' (SC^B 14-15:2) – is released:

Mi Amado, las montañas,	My Beloved, the mountains,
los valles solitarios nemorosos,	lonely wooded valleys,
las ínsulas extrañas,	rare islands,
los ríos sonorosos,	thundering rivers,
el silbo de los aires amorosos,	the whisper of love, carried by the breeze,
la noche sosegada en par de los levantes del aurora,	the tranquil night, at one with the rising dawn,
la música callada,	silent music,
la soledad sonora,	resounding solitude,
la cena que recrea y enamora.	the supper that renews the heart in love.

(SC^B, stanzas 14-15)

The Prologue to *The Spiritual Canticle* emphasises that any attempt to comment is going to look pale. Nevertheless, two things are worth noting.

Firstly, we have here John's testimony to the way God is. These two stanzas of 'Canticle' are like the first news home: the first fruits, freshly cut, from the orchard of John's experience, before our fears and assumptions could turn them stale. Here we have the real horizon of our prayer: all the promise of creation, the intimations of joy that we scarcely dare to hope in, all this the Beloved *is* for us.

> Mountains are high, vast, immense, beautiful, fair, decked with flowers and circled with fragrance: my Beloved is these mountains for me... Valleys...are silent, lovely in their shade and morning freshness, flowing with sweet water... my Beloved is these valleys for me... (SC[B] 14-15:6-7)

Here is access to the centre of John's relationship with the God he has come to know – a God who comes, surprising, unconstrained, and gives all, filling all our potential for loving: You have been this to me; you are this for them.

Secondly, one cannot miss the sense of wonder in John's language: wonder at the sheer presence of the Beloved; that he is, and here, and for me.

In particular, these stanzas convey a sense of breathlessness: there is no verb, no time for a verb, rather a series of word-splashes, a breathless response to a light that is eye-close. This is akin to the 'O' of the 'Living Flame' poem – an exclamation that for the poet spells wonder and praise.[8]

On the other hand, the lines are rich in colour. Up to this point, the bride's anxious search for her Beloved has been all movement and endeavour. Rarely have adjectives been allowed to embellish the story.[9] Now, born of God's disclosure, there is a torrent of description (*wooded* valleys; *rare* islands; *thundering* rivers...), spraying colours across the canvas. John's wonder is confident, radiant, like a bride whose smile blesses the guests because she knows herself accepted in the other's heart.

When John speaks of contemplative prayer, it is a case of a journey (albeit costly) into this: into freedom, into wonder. Growth in prayer means growth in presence. So prayer is likely to become simpler, because fuller; darker, because all-encompassing. This is God's total presence making the person whole; light and love that are met by loving attentiveness:

> In this state God is the agent...; he is giving her blessings at the level of spirit, that is, loving knowledge, his own knowledge and love together... Then the soul too should go on just in loving attentiveness to God,...like someone opening their eyes in the attentiveness of love... (LF 3:32-33)[10]

Simple and open loving attentiveness. Childlike wonder at unearned disclosure. Contemplative prayer means living in a world addressed.

Getting in touch with the real world

In this horizon, the universe looks different. People and events have a different weight.

There is a telling account of John's tact as superior in Segovia, during the last three years of his life:

> Some of the friars he had in his house were not the most perfect or peaceful in the order. Other superiors had found them difficult to deal with. All sought to remove them from their communities in order to preserve a high level of community life... The venerable Father received and welcomed all of these into his house, and with deep feelings of true charity he attended to them...[11]

'Oh – send him to John of the Cross. *He* won't mind...' There is evidence here of someone who sees beneath the gauche exterior; who reads creation in a different way. The awkward, unsightly and smelly in fact came to him from the hand of 'the merciful and all-powerful Father' (LF 2:16). Known in God, creation reveals its splendour (cf. LF 4:4-9).

John's severe-sounding language about the nothingness of creation fits here. It rests on his sense of the delicacy of the universe, 'the sheer dependence, almost the precariousness' of existence.[12] For John, the created universe, from the slightest inflection of a thought to the course of a comet, is being given its being by Another. It exists, because Another is looking at it. The world is *that* childlike: total dependence on the sustaining breath of God. Constantly we are being held out of disintegration by the loving gaze of our Father.

Hence John's language: to love creation apart from God, outside of God, in opposition to God – with 'disordered longing' – is really to commit it to nothingness, to make it supremely ugly.[13] To love creation in God is to be part of something supremely tender.

Creation – the mountains round Granada; the night sky at Segovia; philosophy at Salamanca; gaolers, lice and nightmares in Toledo – is in fact bathed, held, in the gaze of John's Beloved, and cannot but be a motive for praise:

Mil gracias derramando	Pouring out a thousand graces
pasó por estos sotos con presura,	he passed this way in haste;
y, yéndolos mirando,	he cast his gaze across the woodland
con sola su figura	bathed it with his face,
vestidos los dejó de hermosura.	and left it draped in beauty.

(SC, stanza 5)

71

John's vision of things connects us with the real world.

Grace from the inside

In the fullness of union which the second half of 'Canticle' conveys (cf. SC[B], stanzas 22-35), the Beloved's first gift to the bride is insight into the love of the Crucified. She understands a drama in which she has long been involved. The betrothal she now enjoys in fact was hers in baptism, and baptism communicated the content of the Cross. The Bridegroom says to her:

Debajo del manzano,	Beneath the apple tree,
allí conmigo fuiste	there it was that you
desposada,	became my bride.
allí te di la mano	I gave you there my hand
y fuiste reparada	and in that place
donde tu madre fuera	restored you;
violada.	your mother's violation
	is redeemed.

(SC[B], stanza 23)

Commenting, John declares that Jesus' mystery and the Church's sacraments are *the* place of betrothal. What *Canticle* does is show this betrothal working itself out, in a particularly gifted way, across a person's lifetime. 'It is all one; but this [the betrothal in *Canticle*] happens at the soul's pace, and so, little by little; that [on the

72

Cross and in the font], at God's pace, and so all at once' (SC[B] 23:6; cf. 23:3).

We have seen so far that John's central gift is his testimony to the way God is: pressing in to fill him. From there, he could read creation in its proper light, held in the hand of the Beloved. Now we want to emphasise that this horizon is our horizon. 'Mysticism is the interiority of faith.'[14] Mysticism is grace unfolded.

Traditionally, grace comprises two dimensions: God's gift of his Spirit; and his empowering us to enter the Spirit's domain. When God gives, he does not bulldoze, or patronise. He so loves as to make us capable of being part of his love. Faith, charity, is sharing God's life; not just receiving handouts and remaining a stranger.

If that is the 'interiority of faith', John of the Cross puts us inside that 'interior', and enables us, through his testimony, to taste in some way the reality of what we say we believe.

En la interior bodega… In SC[B], stanza 26, John takes us into 'the inner wine cellar'. Here, wine has no additives. God is being permitted to be, at last, 'what He wants to be':[15]

God communicates himself to the soul in this inner union with such a real love, that no mother has ever cherished or caressed her child so tenderly; with this love of God no brother's love or friend's friendship could compare.

So tender and so real is the love of the all-encompassing Father that – how awesome this is, how amazing, what a wonder! – he truly submits himself to this humble, loving soul, so as to make her great, making her great in the kindness he shows her. It is as if he were her servant and she his Lord... So profound is God's humility and gentleness!... 'he will gird himself and have them sit at table, and he will come and serve them.' (SC^B 27:1; cf. Lk 12:37)

This is grace from the inside. For God to love is to give, to give himself, and so to share, and empower. And what this evokes in John is, precisely, wonder.

'O souls created for this greatness and summoned to it! What are you doing?' (SC^B 39:7). Knowing God like this, John cannot remain impassive. Wonder, gratitude, initiates a different way. His testimony invites us to shift from career to partnership, to marriage. His is not a lonely trudge through sludge, but an ice-skating duet, where each moment of the movement comes from the other's pulse.

Praise, gratitude, promote such a shift. They bathe life in a different perspective. John invites us to choose the love of the Son who betroths on the Cross; to choose the love of the Father who risks such disclosure. This is a season of prayer to which John invites us: even when feelings are numb or confused, to 'say and sing', in faith, 'the greatness of the Beloved'.[16]

Epilogue
The Fatherhood of God: A Limitless Embrace

Thinking of Jesus, how do we picture him? St Luke includes this portrait: 'At that time, he rejoiced in the Holy Spirit' — Jesus, alive with joy. His joy is 'in the Holy Spirit': in the love with which his Father fills him. So, he exclaims: 'I thank you, Father, Lord of heaven and earth...' Jesus' joy is pure because it is selfless, dedicated to the Other and gathering in others: 'for you have hidden these things from the learned...and revealed them to little ones' (Lk 10:21). That is the picture: a Jesus whose joy is that others should know the one who is everything to him.

It is hard to speak of this. Human happiness is so partial and inconstant, while God's is all-holy. So here the mystics help. They show that Jesus' communion with 'Abba' is sacred, yet open to ourselves. John of the Cross is one of those 'little ones': he has known Christ's joy, takes us to where Christ stands, and directs our gaze with Christ into the Father's heart, rejoicing in the Father's 'limitless embrace' (LF 1:15).

Painting the walls of the mind

Eau de Nil serenity, the uplift of sunshine breeze, or a normalising magnolia, the colour of one's bedroom does have an influence. But more determining is the paintwork of the mind, the emotional shades one chooses for the heart. On this our spiritual survival can depend. John of the Cross, imprisoned in a squalid boxroom, with black and damp hemming him in, chose beautiful colours for the walls of his heart. The 'Romances on the Trinity' and 'The Spiritual Canticle' are his prison masterpieces: the latter, a song of love; the nine 'Romances', a defining statement of faith. In such an oppressive setting, his faith showed him the Trinity, a canvas dancing with light: a Father who gives his whole self to his Son, a Son surrendered to his Father, a Spirit whose love is more spontaneous the more intense it is:

> As beloved in the lover,
> the one lived in the other...
> for love, the more it is one,
> so much the more does it love. (R 1)

Like a father's pride on prize day, or a husband or wife at their golden wedding anniversary, the Father's delight is tender and radiant:

> Nothing makes me happy, Son,
> if you are not there with me,

and if something does content me,
I love it in you alone…
I find my home in none but you,
O life of my own life…
image of my substance,
in whom is all my joy. (R 2)

The Son, in turn, displays his passion for the
Father as he accepts the Church as bride:

I thank you greatly, Father
– the Son to him replied –;
on the bride you are to give me
my radiance I shall bestow,
so she may perceive
how great you are, my Father,
and how my very being
is pure gift from you. (R 3)

Imprisoned in a 'hollow in a wall',[1] John chose his
way into a different environment: the Son whose
eyes are bright in his Father's gaze. John – and we
– can enter this, because the Son has come down
to our confinement and unlocked there the doors
of our souls.

'From whom' and 'to whom'

The Father whom Jesus reveals is the one 'from
whom' and 'to whom' Jesus is (cf. Jn 8:14). The
world's salvation happens at this point, where
God is known as origin and goal: 'I came from

the Father and have come into the world; and now I am leaving the world and going to the Father' (Jn 16:28). Placing us where Christ stands, John of the Cross helps us receive in gratitude, and journey on pilgrimage. Within God, the Father is eternal source. The Father 'always has conceived [the Word] / and forever he conceives him' (R 1).

Eternally begetting 'within' God, the Father is seen as creator, origin, of all that is 'outside' God. John's other prison poem, on the *fountain* which flows even at night-time, proposes the Father as the all-encompassing wellspring. The universe is not left to sweat it out alone, but is washed in God's lifestream – such abundant waters that they keep 'the underworld, the heavens, and all the nations' from wilting (P 8:6). Hence the poet's wonder at the godliness of creation:

Pouring out a thousand graces
he passed this way in haste;
he cast his gaze across the woodland
bathed it with his face,
and left it draped in beauty. (SC, stanza 5)[2]

For John, the world exists because it is *seen*. It is beautiful, because the Father watches it. It is seen in the Son; its beauty is Christlike. And so it is pleasing to the Father. As the Father initiates creation through the Word, so he originates salvation through Jesus. Jesus is the defining sign of God's fatherliness, of just how much God 'originates' life. That is why no other sign, however supernatural, must be preferred to him. 'In giving us, as he has, his Son, who is his only Word, for he has no other, he has spoken it all to us at once... Set your eyes on him alone' (2A 22:3.5). Jesus is proof that God is infinite gift.

'Our Father'

John's doctrine on prayer derives from this view of God's fatherliness: God as self-giving, generating, outflowing. Growth in prayer lets God be more himself with us. When the person 'sets her happiness in him alone', 'God testifies to *who he is*' (3A 32:2); when God 'sets his favour upon' a soul, 'he is acting *as God*, to show *who he is*' (SC[B] 33:8; cf. LF 3:6).

The ascent up the mountain leads us from the level of sense, faith lived on our terms, to spirit, where God's light comes less refracted. 'For contemplation is nothing other than a secret, peaceful, loving inflowing of God, which, if space is given for this, inflames the soul in the spirit of love' (1DN 10:6) – an exchange, this time, in God's own idiom: 'pure spirit to pure spirit' (2DN 17:4). What the Father does is bestow: he bestows himself on the Son, and in the Son on creation. Contemplation is prayer where this self-givenness of God presides; it is knowing God as Father.

Knowing God's fatherhood like this has consequences. Firstly, it makes other people more important. However unattractive, irritating or different a person may seem, he or she is coming as a gift of the Father, and so at core as 'a most beautiful and accomplished image of God' (1A 9:1). Contemplative prayer and dedicated love for people are inseparable.

Sr Francisca de la Madre de Dios explained John's unbiased kindness by quoting a saying of his: 'wherever we might be, we should do good to all, and show ourselves *children of God*'; we should never 'cause our neighbour offence, either by word or action'. It is about the kind of person one is becoming: 'every time we grew slack on this point, we were doing ourselves more harm than our neighbour.'[3]

Secondly, God's fatherliness requires the Church to be, above all, receptive. If God is bestowing himself, the Church needs hands empty and open to receive. Otherwise, says John, 'as she goes to God, so does she leave, her hands already full and unable to take what God was giving. God deliver us from such sorry burdens which impede such sweet and wholesome freedom!'[4] The key is not a foolproof game plan, but a child's humility and trust.

The journey to the Father's house

Knowing God as Father means receiving all from him. It also means directing all towards him. 'The whole of the Christian life is like a great *pilgrimage to the house of the Father*, whose unconditional love for every human creature...we discover anew each day.'[5] John helps us here, too: to recognise the profound momentum in our lives that is drawing us towards the Father's heart.

Elizabeth was a young novice in Segovia, treated by Fray Juan with fatherly affection. Once he asked her, 'Sister Elizabeth, do you love me?' Wanting to say, 'Yes, hugely', she searched for her best adverb, and came up with, 'Yes, Father, I love you *superciliously*.' This tickled John no end, and he asked her again: 'So, my daughter, you love me *superciliously*?' 'Yes, Father,' she said, all satisfied. The friar replied, 'Well, I love you very much because you are predestined.'[6] John's answer might sound a bit flat, but it is deeply felt: You have been dreamt of by the Father. Courage! God's plan for you exceeds your most daring longings.

At the climax of *Canticle*, this eternal plan spreads out like a glorious landscape. In this 'predestination', 'the Father has gone before the just, blessing them with his gentleness, in his Son Jesus Christ' (SC[B] 37:6). God has not improvised our salvation: he has, from the beginning, seen in us the masterpiece he means us to become.[7]

Sugar on cornflakes

As small children, my sister and I were once asked what God was like. I began describing his black beard and short hair, when my sister chipped in: 'God is like the sugar on your cornflakes: you know it is there, even though you can't see it.' John of the Cross delighted in Fray Francisco's answer to the same question: 'God is what He wants to be.'[8]

Journeying into the Father means entering the unknown. The water which flows by night is a current which 'none can fathom' (P 8:4; cf. Ez 47:5). The *Canticle* question 'Where have you hidden...?' responds to the truth of things. The Son of God is 'hidden' in 'the heart of the Father, the very being of God, which is foreign to mortal eye and hidden from all human understanding' (SC[B] 1:3; cf. Jn 1:18).

So, in praying 'Our Father', we move into mystery and freedom. We may taste, but we cannot see; know, but not describe. 'Of God himself nothing could be said that would be like him' (SC[B] 26:4). Mystical language arises here, in veneration rather than definition. 'The Father spoke one Word, who was his Son, and this he always speaks in eternal silence, and in silence must it be heard by the soul' (SLL 100). Entry into the kingdom goes by way not of working out but of surrender; by way of believing, and of not-understanding (cf. LF 3:48).

This all means that the pilgrimage to the

Father's house can be disconcerting: like a night journey to new lands by paths one has never used before. This 'reversal' – where religion, instead of accommodating the divine to us, is perplexed by the unexpectedness of God – educates the soul in 'courtesy' (1DN 12:3). John looks here to eloquent Job who, when exposed in truth to God, was overcome by silence (cf. Jb 40:3-5); and to Moses, whose knowing meant his removing his sandals and hiding his face.[9]

Jesus has gone to these places. In his aloneness on the cross – 'My God, why...?' – the Son of God included in his relationship with his Father all our dryness, confusion, incapacity, before the divine mystery (cf. 2A 7:11-12). He consecrated it, folded it into his return to the Father's house. Those bewildered by a Father who is not just at their disposal are accompanied by the derelict Christ, reassuring and strengthening them.

The force of delicacy

John of the Cross, then, reveals a God who is very different from us. But he is different, surprising, greater, particularly in his tenderness. 'Father, you show your almighty power in your mercy and forgiveness.'[10] The unfathomable abyss into which our pilgrimage leads is an abyss of kindness. John is amazed at how, in God, power and compassion are one.

This is 'the compassionate and all-powerful Father' (LF 2:16), whose touch is 'all the stronger and more powerful, the more delicate it is' (LF 2:18); he is 'the immense Father' (SC^B 27:1), whose affection for his children is more tender than that of any mother. 'How amazing! How worthy of wonder and dread!' John exclaims, considering not God's dominion, but the Father's 'humility and gentleness' in serving the soul (SC^B 27:1).

God's infinity is the servant of his love. The second stanza of 'The Living Flame' expresses this brilliantly. The Father transforms us through the Spirit of his Son: the hand touches with a fire that heals. Addressing the Father, the 'gentle hand', John comments: 'But you, O life divine, you never slay except to give life; you never wound except to heal. When you chastise, you touch lightly, and this itself could burn up the world. But when it comes to showing kindness, you lay your hand most firmly, and so the bliss of your gentleness knows no bounds' (LF 2:16).

Children in the Son

When Jesus said, 'Father', he could 'rejoice' because he was allowing the fulfilment of all his Father's longing to love. The Father 'rests', indeed 'fits', only in the Son (cf. SC^B 1:5). Jesus could 'rejoice' because the infinite force of his love was being received in the 'limitless embrace' of the

Father's 'kindness' (LF 1:15). That is where John came to live, in the love uniting Son and Father.

All the baptised belong there, rising from the font to hear: 'You are my beloved child; with you I am well pleased' (cf. Lk 3:22).[11] In a brittle world, there is a need for people who have learned to live in the Father's embrace. John's living there spread calm and warmth, hope and courage. So testifies Fray Martín: John 'was so loved by his subjects as if he were each one's father.'[12]

Notes

Foreword

1. The six main sections of this book – Biographical Introduction, Chapters 1-4 and Epilogue – first appeared in the following issues of *Mount Carmel: A Review of the Spiritual Life* respectively: vols. 38/4 (1990), 50/2 (2002), 47/2 (1999), 48/2 (2000), 47/4 (2000) and 54/3 (2006).

Biographical Introduction

1. Lucas de San José, OCD, in Crisógono de Jesús Sacramentado, OCD, *Vida de San Juan de la Cruz*, Madrid: Biblioteca de Autores Cristianos, 1982, p. 413, note 31.
2. Lt 26, to Mother María de la Encarnación, July 6, 1591.
3. Lt 31, to Ana de Peñalosa, September 21, 1591.

Chapter 1

1. Lt 20, to a Carmelite nun, shortly before Pentecost, 1590.

2. Jerónimo de la Cruz, OCD, in Crisógono de Jesús Sacramentado, OCD, *op. cit.*, p. 264, note 87.

3. In the sense of making a decision (with good discernment). See Javier Melloni, SJ, *The Exercises of St Ignatius Loyola in the Western Tradition*, Leominster: Gracewing / New Malden: Inigo, 2000, p. 51.

4. In SC^B. This stanza is absent from SC^A.

5. Already a catchphrase in sixteenth-century spirituality.

6. *agradar a Dios* (3A 35:7); see also 3A 28:8; 30:5; 1DN 3:2; 6:6; 2DN 19:4.

7. *Good News Bible: Today's English Version.*

8. Note this description by the bride in *Canticle* of the enamoured soul: *penado en la ausencia* (SC^B 1:21); and of Christ in the 'Shepherd' song: *solo... penado... ausencia* (P 7:1.4).

9. Jean Vanier, *Becoming Human*, London: Darton, Longman & Todd, 1999, pp. 20-1 & 26.

10. Pope Benedict XVI (as Cardinal Joseph Ratzinger), *In the Beginning*, Edinburgh: T&T Clark, 1995, p. 74.

11. Pope John Paul II, *Evangelium Vitae* (*On the Value and Inviolability of Human Life*), Encyclical Letter, March 25, 1995, # 19.

12. Lt 8, to the Carmelite sisters of Beas, November 22, 1587.

Chapter 2

1. José de Jesús María, OCD, *Vida de San Juan de la Cruz* III, Burgos: El Monte Carmelo, 1927, p. 451, quoted in Maximiliano Herráiz, OCD (ed.), *San Juan de la Cruz: Obras Completas*, Salamanca: Ediciones Sígueme, 1992, p. 16.

2. Magdalena del Espíritu Santo, OCD, *Relación*, in *Biblioteca Mística Carmelitana*, Burgos: El Monte Carmelo, 1931, vol. X, p. 324, quoted in Herráiz (ed.), *op. cit.*, p. 16.

3. See Monika K Hellwig, *The Eucharist and the Hunger of the World*, Kansas City, MO: Sheed & Ward, 1992, p. 5.

4. I am regarding all nine of these 'Romances' as composed in Toledo, though there is debate about this.

Chapter 3

1. See 3A 1:1 which speaks of these three 'powers of the soul' or 'faculties' depending on each other.

2. My italics; in Spanish: *perfeccionar*; *enterar.*

3. The term *metánoia* 'literally means to allow the spirit to be overturned in order to make it turn towards God': see John Paul II, *Reconciliatio et Paenitentia* (*On Reconciliation and Penance in the Mission of the Church Today*), Apostolic Exhortation, December 2, 1984, # 26. The phrase

'change your way of thinking' is an expression of the biblical scholar Raymond Brown.

4. This is in line with the cheerful philosophy of the Middle Ages. See, for example, Josef Pieper, *Leisure: The Basis of Culture*, London: Fontana, 1965.

5. Fragment 112, quoted in *ibid.*, p. 27.

6. Henri de Lubac, SJ, *The Splendour of the Church*, San Francisco: Ignatius Press, 1992, p. 251.

7. See also 2A 17:9. In 2A 19 John invites a deeper reception of the word in Scripture. Receive it not at the level of the *letter* – that is, of *sense*, surface (*corteza*), the narrowness of one's own mindset; receive it rather at the level of *spirit*, which is far more 'abundant' (cf. 2A 19:5). For their part, spiritual directors should draw the person's attention away from any supernatural experiences she might have, encouraging her to stay 'in the freedom and darkness of faith, in which one receives the freedom and abundance of spirit' (2A 19:11).

8. See Foreword to Terry Waite, *Taken on Trust*, London: Hodder & Stoughton, 1993.

Chapter 4

1. In Federico Ruiz, OCD et al., *God Speaks in the Night: The Life, Times, and Teaching of St. John of the Cross*, Washington, DC: ICS Publications, 2000, p. 234.

2. Hans Urs von Balthasar develops this beautifully: see his *Prayer*, San Francisco: Ignatius Press, 1986, pp. 38-9.

3. Lt 260:1, to Gracián, August 21-22, 1578; Teresa goes on, in this letter, to express envy at John's 'martyrdom' (Lt 260:2).

4. Lt 233:3, to Gracián, March 10-11, 1578.

5. See 2DN 13:5; cf. 2DN 7; also 2DN 5:1; 2DN 10.

6. The three quotations are from: Ps 76:14/77:13 (in 2A 8:3); 1DN 12:3; SC^B 26:4.

7. As expressed by Jean Vanier in an address in Sligo, 1996.

8. *estimación*; *encarecimiento*: in LF 2:5; cf. 2:15.

9. Only in SC^A, stanza 11 (SC^B, stanza 12) – *cristalina fuente* – do adjectives appear: see Dámaso Alonso, in Colin P Thompson, *The Poet and the Mystic: A Study of the Cántico Espiritual of San Juan de la Cruz*, Oxford: Oxford University Press, 1977, p. 82.

10. See also 2A 12:7-8; 1DN 9:8; SC^B 16:11; 39:12.

11. Testimony of Jerónimo de San José, OCD, in Ruiz et al., *God Speaks in the Night*, *op. cit.*, p. 329.

12. Ross Collings, OCD, *John of the Cross*, Collegeville, MN: The Liturgical Press, 1990, p. 31. See all of his Chapter 2, 'Creation – "By the hand of the Beloved"'.

13. 'compared with' (1A 4:4); put 'in a balance with God' (1A 5:4); *acto desordenado del apetito* (1A 6:1).

14. Henri de Lubac, SJ, 'Mysticism and Mystery', in his *Theological Fragments*, San Francisco: Ignatius Press, 1989, p. 56.

15. See note 1.

16. To recall words from near the beginning of this chapter: cf. SC[B] 14-15:2.

Epilogue

1. This is how Inocencio de San Andrés describes John's Toledo dungeon: in *Biblioteca Mística Carmelitana*, *op. cit.*, vol. XIV, p. 66.

2. For the Spanish of SC, stanza 5, see p. 71.

3. In *Biblioteca Mística Carmelitana*, *op. cit.*, vol. XIV, p. 172.

4. Lt 7, to the nuns at Beas, November 18, 1586.

5. John Paul II, *Tertio Millennio Adveniente* (*On Preparation for the Jubilee of the Year 2000*), Apostolic Letter, November 10, 1994, # 49.

6. See José Vicente Rodríguez, OCD, *Florecillas de San Juan de la Cruz*, Madrid: Ediciones Paulinas, 1990, p. 98.

7. Cf. II Council of Orange, Can. 12, DS 382: 'God loves us as we shall be through his gift; not as we are through our own merit.'

8. In Ruiz et al., *God Speaks in the Night*, *op. cit.*, p. 234.

9. See 1DN 12:3; Ex 3:5-6; cf. 1DN 8:3; 2DN 16:8.

10. Opening Prayer at Mass for Sunday, Week 26, in *The Sunday Missal*, London: Collins, 1975, p. 356.

11. Cf. John Paul II, *Christifideles Laici* (*On the Vocation and the Mission of the Lay Faithful in the Church and in the World*), Apostolic Exhortation, December 30, 1988, # 11.

12. Fray Martín de San José, OCD, in *Biblioteca Mística Carmelitana*, *op. cit.*, vol. XIV, p. 13.

TERESIAN PRESS
PUBLICATIONS AVAILABLE

The Writings of St Teresa of Avila: An Introduction
Eugene McCaffrey, OCD
£5.00

John of the Cross: Seasons of Prayer
Iain Matthew, OCD
£5.00

Infinite Horizons: Scripture through Carmelite Eyes
James McCaffrey, OCD
£8.00

Elizabeth of the Trinity: The Unfolding of her Message
Joanne Mosley
2 volumes, £10.00 each volume

Holiness For All: Themes from St Thérèse of Lisieux
Aloysius Rego, OCD
£7.00

Upon This Mountain: Prayer in the Carmelite Tradition
Mary McCormack, OCD
£4.00

Let Yourself Be Loved: Elizabeth of the Trinity
Eugene McCaffrey, OCD
£5.00

Teresian Press
Carmelite Priory
Boars Hill
Oxford OX1 5HB

www.carmelitebooks.com

TERESIAN PRESS
SOME FORTHCOMING PUBLICATIONS

St Teresa on Prayer: Exploring The Way of Perfection
Jerome Lantry, OCD

Living with God: St Teresa's Understanding of Prayer
Tomás Álvarez, OCD

A Moment of Prayer – A Life of Prayer
Conrad De Meester, OCD

The Our Father: St Teresa of Avila's Catechism of Prayer
Aloysius Rego, OCD

*Captive Flames: A Biblical Reading of
the Carmelite Saints – to be reissued*
James McCaffrey, OCD

*Journey of Love: Teresa of Avila's Interior Castle
– A Reader's Guide*
Eugene McCaffrey, OCD

What Carmel Means to Me
Edited by James McCaffrey, OCD & Joanne Mosley

Teresian Press
Carmelite Priory
Boars Hill
Oxford OX1 5HB

www.carmelitebooks.com